How to Start Your Own Rental Property Business

Buying Multi Family Homes & Rental Real Estate Financing

By Ferguson Greene

Table of Contents

DEDICATION

This book is dedicated to my son's
Christian and Matthew.
A blessing from God and the joy of my life.

ACKNOWLEDGMENTS

I WOULD LIKE TO ACKNOWLEDGE ALL THE
HARD WORK OF THE MEN AND WOMEN OF THE
UNITED STATES MILITARY, WHO RISK THEIR
LIVES ON A DAILY BASIS, TO MAKE THE WORLD
A SAFER PLACE.

Disclaimer

This book was written as a guide to starting a business. As with any other high yielding action, starting a business has a certain degree of risk. This book is not meant to take the place of accounting, legal, financial or other professional advice. If advice is needed in any of these fields, you are advised to seek the services of a professional.

While the author has attempted to make the information in this book as accurate as possible, no guarantee is given as to the accuracy or currency of any individual item. Laws and procedures related to business are constantly changing.

Therefore, in no event shall Brian Mahoney or MahoneyProducts Publishers be liable for any special indirect, or consequential damages or any damages whatsoever in connection with the use of the information herein provided.

Chapter 1

Rental Property Investing Overview

Rental Property Investing Overview

Rental Property Investing is purchasing investment property for the purpose of renting it out for positive cash flow. It can be single family homes, mulitifamily units, apartment complexes or commercial property.

One of the biggest advantages of rental property investing, is getting passive income. Having your property or investment work for you, and earn a income while you relax or move on to other projects. If done properly, rental property investing can give you the freedom to live life on your terms and set your own schedule.

Rental Property Investing advantages:

* You don't have to be present to make money. You can purchase a home and have the rest of the work subcontracted out, and earn positive cash flow.

* Rental property investing allows you to make money in a variety of ways. You can earn appreciation on your property value and have your equity grow. You get tax benefits, interest and business write offs for property ownership. You can get positive cash flow income from your tenant's rent.

* You have a variety of business models to choose from. Single Family, Mulitfamily or Commercial property.

Rental Property Investing Overview

* Real Estate Investing is one of the most sound and enduring businesses ever created. When I was a child, JC Penny's and Sears were the retail giants. They have been replaced by Amazon and Walmart. Real Estate investing however, will always be around because people will always need a place to stay.

* The principles for success are easy to understand. Buy at or below wholesale, rehab if necessary, rent or flip for a profit.

When you start a rental property business, begin with the end in mind. What strategy do you want to use? There are several types of strategies to decide on. For example:

* What type of property do you want to invest in? Single family, multifamily, commercial lease, apartments, condos or duplexes?

* How much money do you want to earn? Knowing that number will help you to decide what type of property you want to invest in.

* How will you finance your properties? High interest loans from private lenders? Deal with the regulation of traditional lenders or how about using credit cards?

Rental Property Investing Overview

* Where do you want to invest? Many suggest you start out, witnin one hour of where you live. But if you have really big financial goals, you may decide to invest nationwide.

* What is your time frame? "Dreams are goals with a deadline." Tony Robbins. You have to make a list of goals that are accompanied with deadlines.

* Are you going to manage your properties or hire a property management company?

* All business ventures involve risk. Expect the best, prepare for the worst. Business liability insurance will help, as well as the decisions you make involving financing and tenant selection.

* Vacancy. Eventually a tenant will move out. What model of marketing will you use to buffer the lost of a tenant.

* Passive income is not passive, if you are working on everything. How much are you going to delegate or subcontract out?

Once you select your overall rental property investment strategies you have to put a team together. You will need an attorney, accountant, real estate agent, repair man or maintenance person and a marketing person.

When you select an attorney make sure he or she specializes in real estate. They have to have a detailed knowledge of real estate contracts that are fair and protect you.

When it comes to accounting there are tons of software options out there that might persuade you to do your own accounting. You have to decide how much responsibility you want to have when it comes to accounting.

If you have a good real estate agent, they are well worth their commission. The best real estate agents work full time. They are more motivated because their dinner depends on their success. They should be able to give you accurate comps (comps is short for Comparables. It is a real estate appraisal term referring to properties that are similar, that have sold recently in the same area) and have a deep understanding of the real estate market.

Whether it's a single family, or much larger property, you should have a maintenance or repair person. Depending on the size of your business, you may need to have several maintenance personnel. If you decide to hire subcontractors, use references to make sure they are reliable.

Marketing. With the growth of the internet, there are now tons of ways to market your property. Your marketing can be as simple as business cards and a web site. Or your marketing could also be as detailed as creating YouTube videos for marketing in combination with other forms of social media like Facebook Ads, email marketing, customer list building, article marketing and press releases.

"Study to show yourself approved, a workman that need not be ashamed." Make educated decisions based on sound knowledge (people are destroyed for lack of knowledge). Learn from your mistakes.

Practice patiences for your success. In the parable of the Chinises bamboo tree, speaker Les Brown teaches that the Chinese baboo tree has to be watered every day while it grows for 5 years underground. Then it reaches enormous heights, shortly after it bursts threw the ground. Continue to water your real estate dreams for your breaktrhrough.

Make a decision to be determined to succeed. Set your goals. Make a plan. Then take action. Nothing worthwile comes without challenges. Learn to enjoy the challenges, knowing that it is helping you to grow. After all, what's life without a little adventure?

Chapter 2
Property Management
Business Overview

Property Management

A Property Manager manages real estate both commercial and residential. His or her responsibilities are vast. A property manager could oversee and monitor...

* Getting a license

* Finding a property

* Purchasing a property

* Marketing to bring tenants into the properties

* Collecting rent & security deposits from tenants

* Getting Rental Contracts made and signed

* Employees and contracts

* Screen prospective tenants

* Dealing with problem tenants

* Moving out tenants

* Handling tenant complaints

* Maintenance of properties and contractors

* Keeping the Properties clean

* Property security

* Financial Management and record keeping

Most states require property management companies to be licensed.

The courses below can help train real estate professionals for a license.

National Apartment Association Education Institute (NAAEI)

https://www.naahq.org/about/naaei

This National Apartment Association also provides education courses and certifications for professionals in the apartment industry.

The National Apartment Association Education Institute (NAAEI) offers these courses. NAAEI is the education arm of NAA. It provides a large-based education, training and recruitment programs to develop apartment industry leaders.

https://www.naahq.org/education-careers/find-a-course

Courses Offered

* Certified Apartment Manager (CAM)

* Certified Apartment Portfolio Supervisor (CAPS)

* Certificate for Apartment Maintenance Technicians (CAMT)

* Independent Rental Owner Professional Designation Course (IROP)

* National Apartment Leasing Professional (NALP)

Start-up Cost: $3,000-$5,000

Potential Earnings: $25,000-$50,000

Typical Fees:

$25 per hour or monthly retainer $500-$2,500

Advertising:

Zero Cost Online Marketing, Internet Marketing, Business Cards, Online classified ads, Website

Qualifications:

Experience in Property Management or college degree or certification in the field. Management & communication skills, bookkeeping & building maintenance knowledge.

Equipment Needed:

Computer, spreadsheet & management software, printer, internet access, wi-fi, phone.

Home Business Potential: Yes

Staff Required: No

Hidden Costs: Insurance Bonding

Business Models

Percentage of rent

When the Percentage of rent model is used the management company gets between 10-15% of the rent. This model is the most frequently used.

Fixed fee

If a house, land or property is vacant and being monitered, then the Fixed fee model is most frequently used.

Guaranteed rent

When you have small units that are in great demand the Guranteed rent model is the most frequently used. The owner of the property signs a agreement with the management company and reguardless of the rent, pays a fixed fee.

Revenue share

Revenue share is an agreement that is usually done with commercial properties like apartment complexes and business locations. The owner and property manager share the risk in a revenue generating idea and after sharing the revenue for a fixed time, the owner gets all or most of the revenue.

CHAPTER 3

Finding Wholesale Investment Property

How to Find Wholesale Residential & Commercial Real Estate

How To Find Wholesale Real Estate

There are several basic methods to find real estate at wholesale prices. There are foreclosures and pre-foreclosures, so get excited! There are hundreds of great deals just waiting for you to find them! The first method is Searching Public Records.

Searching Public Records

Go to your county's recorders office and look for notice of default or notice of sale. The advantage of this method is that many newly posted properties have not been seen by your competition. The disadvantage is that it usually takes more time to find property than the other methods.

Here is a tip. When ever a county clerk helps you, get that person's name and thank them face to face. Then go home and call the office and thank them again. Wait about a week. Then purchase a thank you card and mail it. Your kindness is going to stand out to that clerk. In turn that clerk is not likely to forget you. You in turn will likely have an ally in that office. The old saying "It's not what you know, but who you know." This method helps the clerk and yourself get to know each other quicker than usual. At the very least, you should feel good for being a nice person!

How To Find Wholesale Real Estate

Another advantage to searching public records is Probate Properties. You will need to be educated in your local area's probate laws to purchase those properties.

Probate is required for all estates that are not protected by a trust. The average duration of probate is 7 to 8 months.

If the house is owned outright, the estate is responsible for remitting property taxes and insurance premiums throughout the probate process.

Estate administrators can elect to sell the property if it is causing financial harm to the estate. If the estate does not have sufficient funds to cover outstanding debts, the probate judge can order the property sold.

How a probate house is sold depends on the type of probate that is used. "Court Confirmation" is the most common type of probate used. A judge must approve all of the aspects of the management of the estate. Independent Administration of Estate's Act (IAEA) governs the 2nd type of probate administration. It allows estate executors to engage in estate administrative affairs without the court management.

How To Find Wholesale Real Estate

To purchase probate property you have to know which probate system is being applied. Properties can be bought directly from the estate executor when Independent Administration of Estate's process is in effect. You can place your bid through the court system when court approval is required.

An investor interested in finding probate real estate must research public records. When people pass away their last will and testament is recorded in the probate court. The last will and testament will contain valuable information such as the estate assets, who is the beneficiary, and contact info for whoever is administrating for the estate.

Property records should show if there are any liens on the property and if so, who holds the lien. They should also show the properties appraised value, the year it was constructed, the square footage and the lot size. The records may also help you to determine if there have been any tax liens placed on the property.

Do your due diligence when purchasing any type of real estate. Bring in professional help in the form of building inspectors, lawyers and any other professionals that can help protect you when needed.

Using the Internet

I will provide you with a Small Real Estate Rolodex of web sites later in this chapter. Many are completely free and have tons of information. One success algorithm for buying a property is that you should never, never, purchase one property without looking at, at least 100 other properties. Being able to search online makes using this formula very easy.

Using Local Papers and Journals

Local papers and journals. By law many foreclosures have to be posted in the local paper. This can mean a goldmine of opportunity for you. With newspaper circulation in decline, many people are simply not looking in the newspaper anymore. Advantage you.

Next I am going to cover several categories of real estate sources.

* Nationwide banks & Foreclosure Properties

* Government Foreclosure Properties

* Commercial Real Estate

* FSBO - For Sale By Owner

How To Find Wholesale Real Estate

Nationwide Banks & Foreclosure Properties

Bank of America

http://foreclosures.bankofamerica.com/

I have purchased property using this web site. It is my favorite because they have a large nationwide inventory and their web site is easy to navigate and sort properties.

Wells Fargo

https://reo.wellsfargo.com/

Place yourself on their mailing list, and get property updates on a monthly basis.

Ocwen Financial Corporation

http://www.ocwen.com/reo

Founded in 1988 they are one of the largest mortgage companies in America.

Hubzu

http://www.hubzu.com/

Hubzu is a nationwide real estate auction web site. Very easy to use. This is a great web site for comparing property prices nationwide.

How To Find Whoesale Real Estate

Government Foreclosure Properties

One advantage purchasing from the government is that there is no emotional attachment to the property. Don't be afraid to make a offer that is lower than the listed price. I once argued with a real estate agent who refused to place a offer lower than the stated price. Eventually I got him to place the offer. (Remember that they work for you, however some government properties can't be purchased unless you go through a HUD or government approved agent.) It was countered twice, before I decided to purchase another property. But they countered with two offers lower than the listed price.

If you are reading a ebook version of this book then you should be able to access these web sites by clicking the links below. But if you are reading a paperback version of this book then be careful when looking for government properties. There are many web sites pretending to be government web sites and some will attempt to charge you fees for information about government properties.

How To Find Wholesale Real Estate
Government Foreclosure Properties

Fannie Mae
The Federal National Mortgage Association

https://www.fanniemae.com/singlefamily/reo-vendors

Department of Housing and Urban Development

https://www.hudhomestore.com/Home/Index.aspx

The Federal Deposit Insurance Corporation

https://www.fdic.gov/buying/owned/

The United States Department of Agriculture

https://properties.sc.egov.usda.gov/resales/index.jsp

United States Marshals

https://www.usmarshals.gov/assets/sales.htm#real estate

How To Find Wholesale Real Estate

Commercial Real Estate Properties

City Feet

is a nationwide database of Commercial Real Estate Property

http://www.cityfeet.com/#

The Commercial Real Estate Listing Service

is a nationwide database of Commercial Real Estate Property

https://www.cimls.com/

Land . Net

is a nationwide database of land, commercial real estate for sale and for lease.

http://www.land.net/

Loop . Net

is a nationwide database of Commercial Real Estate Property

http://www.loopnet.com/

FSBO – For Sale By Owner

By Owner

http://www.byowner.com/

For sale by owner in Canada

http://www.fsbo-bc.com/

For sale by owner Central

http://www.fsbocentral.com/

For sale by Owner: world's largest FSBO web site

http://www.forsalebyowner.com/

Ranch by owner

http://www.ranchbyowner.com/

CHAPTER 4

REAL ESTATE FINANCING 4,000 Sources!

8 Realistic Ways to Finance Real Estate

Welcome to Expert financing. I am going to show you several realistic ways to finance real estate. You are going to learn how to finance real estate with.

* VA LOANS

* PARTNERS

* INVESTMENT CLUBS

* CREDIT CARDS

* CORPORATE CREDIT

* EQUITY

* SELLER FINANCE

* HARD MONEY LENDERS

* AND FINALLY I SHOW YOU THE MONEY$!!

USING A VA LOAN

According to the web sites www.benefits.va.gov and www.military.com the current VA Loan amount is a whopping $417,000! What a lot of veterans don't know is that you can use that money to purchase not only your home, but investment properties. That is how I started my investing career. Purchasing multiple homes using my VA Loan.

Even if you are not a veteran, you can still partner up with one, who still has some money left on his or her VA LOAN.

If you are a Veteran, you will need to obtain a copy of your DD 214 and VA Form 26-1880 Request for a Certificate of Eligibility.

PARTNERS

This is another way I purchased a home. At the time I worked for the United States Postal Service. I had already purchased plenty of homes, so many of the workers were aware I had successfully invested in real estate. At break time I went around and ask people to partner up with me. I had multiple people offer to go in as a partner. I choose one and that house we rehabbed and flipped just two months after purchasing it. To this day it was the biggest gross profit on one deal, I have had. True I had to split it with my partner, but I would rather have half of something than all of nothing.

Having the combined resources of two people can be a great benefit, but it is not without it's challenges. If you are going to use a partner, no matter how close you are...GET EVERY THING IN WRITING.

FINANCING REAL ESTATE

Having a partner can dramatically increase the chance of a Bank lending money as well as having someone to split the work on rehabbing, should you decide to save money and make repairs yourself. But all this must be spelled out BEFORE you enter into a Agreement/Contract and purchase a home.

It helps if the person is like minded and understands the risks and benefits of investing, and truly understands the return on investment of a particular deal.

REAL ESTATE INVESTMENT CLUBS

Real estate investment clubs are groups that meet locally and allow investors and other professionals to network and learn. They can provide extremely useful information for both the novice and expert real estate investor. A top real estate club can provide a great forum to network, learn about reputable contractors, brokers, realtors, lawyers, accountants and other professionals. On the other hand, there are many real estate clubs designed to sell you. They bring in "gurus" who sell either on stage or at the back of the room, and as a result, the clubs typically profit to the tune of %50 of the sale price of the product, bootcamp, or training that is pitched.

I have purchased a ton of real estate books and real estate courses. Carlton Sheets, Dave Del Dotto, The Mylands, Seminar courses and much much more. I am not against any club bringing in a speaker who has a course. However I think there should be transparency to the members of the club.

There is certainly value in the networking that may come at one of these groups. But attend working to attain your goals and not necessarily the club's goal to sell you something. Some times both are the same thing. As a rule I usually leave debit cards at home the first time I attend an event. If there is a seller there with a "This day only offer" then I won't feel pressured to purchase. Plus most sellers can be convinced to sell at the discount offer price at a later time when you have had a chance to come down off the "sense of urgency emotional pitch" .

CREDIT CARDS

When using a credit card in real estate you must really do your homework on the deal. Dan Kennedy a world famous marketer once said "always stack the numbers in your favor". That's how you use a credit card. Look at the return on investment as compared to the long term cost of using a credit card and it's interest. Also I would recommend buying low cost homes that you can purchase and own free and clear

No Mortgage Payment!!! My last 2 homes I have purchased have been cash deals. One home cost $1,500 and the other about $7,000. The first was a government property from HUD and the 2nd From a Bank. These institutions are unemotional about real estate and simply view a property as a non performing asset. The 2nd home was 4 bedrooms, 1 1/2 bath and a basement located in a farming community and came with a 2 car garage/shed and .6 acre(that is the size of a NFL football field) of land.

In this book I show you how to find plenty of houses with amazing below wholesale prices and a formula for almost always finding a great deal.

CORPORATE CREDIT

Many people set up corporations to buy and sell real estate as an additional protection against liabilities. Other's create a corporation to mask personal involvement in property transfers and public records. Regardless of the use of a corporation, you can buy real estate with corporate credit as an alternative to using your own cash or IRA. By capitalizing on the credit rating of your corporation, you can buy real estate and build your corporate holdings portfolio.

Just remember that you can set up your corporation in a state that favors you the most for your real estate deals. Do your research. Most people like Delaware and Nevada, but you will have to decide if your home state or any other state is best for you and your business.

CURRENT EQUITY

Using the equity in your home for real estate investing is another way you can finance properties. You might use the money for a down payment or it may only be enough to cover the cost of some rehab repairs.

If you stick to the low cost home formula, you may have enough to purchase the entire house. A house is an investment that should appreciate in value as well as give a great ROI (Return On Investment). When you decide to flip the property or rent it out fo positive cashflow.

If you have equity and it's not doing anything, then you may decide to make it a "performing asset" and use it as part of your real estate finance program.

SELLER FINANCING

Seller finance is where the seller of a free and clear property becomes your bank along with being the seller.

Advantages:

You get to purchase the property on terms that may be more beneficial for you. Seller gets monthly payments and the benefit of treating the sale as an installment sale thus allowing them to defer any capital gains taxes that may be due.

Disadvantages:

You may be locked into a mortgage with a pre-payment penalty or may not be able to resell the property immediately. This strategy is typically not meant for flipping but can definitely be used for that purpose if structured correctly.

Seller Finance is a known way to finance a property. That is why I have presented it in this book. But it is my least favorite because you now have a lingering relationship with your property. Your ability to make decisions regarding the property is limited and for that reason, I would not go this route. However, like all types of financing, you have to ask yourself, "is the deal worth it."

I also prefer to work alone, but when a great deal came along, I sought out a partner to make it happen. Risk is usually relative to potential profit.

HARD MONEY LENDERS

A hard money lender is usually a individual or company that lends money for an investment secured by the investment property.

Advantages:

Less red tape to get the money. You are dealing with people who understand the real estate investment business.

Disadvantage:

This is not a long term loan. The lender wants a return on investment, usually within a few months, a a year, or a few years. The interest rate on the loan is much higher than usual conventional banks.

Using hard money has a higher risk because the return on investment is due quicker. Therefore it is a good idea not to use a Hard Money Lender, until you have a great deal of experience and confidence in being able to produce a return on investment.

SHOWING YOU THE MONEY

A list of web sites for financing.

www.businessfinance.com (4,000 sources of money!)

www.advanceamericaproperty.com

http://www.cashadvanceloan.com/

www.brookviewfinancial.com

www.commercialfundingcorp.com

www.dhlc.com
(hard money for the Texas area)

www.equity-funding.com

www.bankofamerica.com

www.carolinahardmoney.com
(for real estate investors in North and South Carolina)

www.fpfloans.com

As you can see there are plenty of strategies for financing a property. Do your research on your investment property and get the true market value. Purchase well below wholesale. This will help to minimize risk and elevate your potential profit margins. Buying below wholesale also creates a buffer for unexpected expenses.

So don't let the lack of money be a roadblock in your real estate investing dreams.

Chapter 5
Managing Your Rental Properties

Keeping the Property Clean

You should have your property always as clean as possible. Curbside appeal can attract new tenants and make the tenants you have, desire to stay.

Have maintanance personnel make a routine inspection of the property to make sure that trash and debris are taken care of.

Larger properties may require a commercial property cleaning service.

Keep your property landscaped and the grass at the proper length. Again this adds to the curb appeal.

Part of keeping your property clean is to have an extermination company keep your property free of unwanted pests, like rodents and roaches.

Property Security

The property should be well lit. Light helps deter crime. However good lighting might not be enough. You may need to hire a security service to patrol the grounds or at least be on call, depending on the crime in the area.

Tenants may move out, if they don't feel safe. So make your tenants feel protected. Having security on property can deter crime and give the tenants a better feeling of comfort.

Managing Your Rental PROPERTIES

Financial Management and Record Keeping

Software

Recently property management software prices have
lowered and that has increased it's popularity.
Software technology is allowing property managers
to save time and run a more efficent business. Below
are some of the top property management software
programs currently on the market. All information,
copy and pricing was taken from their website.

Property management software

123LandLord

http://www.123landlord.com/

**123Landlord allows you to manage all of your tenants and properties,
collect payments and track rent due.**

They Currently have 5 versions.

Free	free	2 tenants	2 properties
Professional	$13 a month	12 tenants	12 properties
Premier	$29 a month	50 tenants	50 properties
Deluxe	$49 a month	75 tenants	75 properties
Enterprise	$79 a month	Unlimited	Unlimited

Financial Management and Record Keeping

Acturent

Forms

Preloaded legal forms save you time and money.

Website

Acturent allows you to build a custom website for your organization at no extra charge.

Tenant Services

Advertise your availabilities online, accept online payments, online applications, and much more...

Offers service and support by email.

They charge a base fee of $5 a month plus .30 cents per unit.

https://acturent.com/

AppFolio

"AppFolio Property Manager is designed for property managers who want to automate, modernize, and grow their business. Whether you manage multifamily, single-family, student housing, HOA, condo, or commercial properties- or maybe you manage a mixed portfolio - our all-in-one cloud-based solution has features built specifically for you so you can streamline your workday and focus on your bottom line."

Residental $1.25 per unit a month

Commercial $1.50 per unit a month

Student Housing $1.25 per unit a month

Community Associations $.80 per unit a month

http://www.appfolio.com/

There are plenty of property management companies, and with modern technology creating better management software, you have plenty of options for managing your rental property.

Chapter 6
Peace of Mind Tenant Rental Property Blueprint

A reminder for all matters and topics in this book consult an attorney or other qualified professionals.

Getting Rental Contracts made and signed

A rental agreement is a short-term contract, usually month to month. It can be written or verbal.

A lease is a written agreement that specifies the length and cost of the rent each month for that period.

You should have an attorney that specializes in lease agreements, make up your contracts.

If you decide to do it yourself here are web site s

that have templates for every state in the United States.

Nationwide Rental Lease Agreements

https://rentalleaseagreements.com/residential/

Rocket Lawyer Free Lease Agreements

https://goo.gl/vQGTEz

BLUEPRINT FOR TENANTS

How to Screen Prospective Tenants

Credit Score

Check the credit score of any prospective tenants. The credit score can show and ability to pay and a willingness to take responsiblity to pay obligations.

Steady Employment

Use paystubs and bank statements as proof of steady employment and the ability to pay.

Income Ratio

Income ratio should be about 3 times the amount of the rent.

Background Check

For your safety and the safety of any other tenants, do not skip on doing a background check.

BLUEPRINT FOR TENANTS

How to Screen Prospective Tenants

Prior Evictions

Check for prior evictions. Make sure another property manager is not trying to pass their problem off on you.

Valid Credentials

Make sure that all identification and credentials match up. Some times people attempt to rent property in other peoples names.

References

Check references thoroughly. Make sure that family and friends are not posing as prior landlords or work supervisors.

Reason for Moving

Ask the prospective tenant what was his reason for moving from his last residence. It may give you some insight into what kind of tenant you are going to have.

BLUEPRINT FOR TENANTS

Money – Money - Money

Collecting rent

There are several ways to collect rent. Below are a few of the more common and popular ones.

Online or ACH

automated clearing house payments

This is by far, the most convenient for you. One such company is Agile Payments.

https://www.agilepayments.com/

Drop Off Box

Just have a secured drop off box at a office on the property grounds.

By Mail

Make sure that the tenant is aware that payment by mail still has to be received by the due date.

BLUEPRINT FOR TENANTS

How to Handle Tenant Complaints

Make sure that tenants must put ALL COMPLAINTS in writing. Letter or email. Make no verbal agreements! Respond to complaints as quickly as possible. Make sure that any contract that responds to any proplem only makes repairs authorized by you.

Common Complaints and How to Handle Them

Neighbor Complaints

Start with a phone call and get the accused side of the story. If that does not work, do a field inspection to verify any complaint. If the complaint is valid, send the accused a letter citing what ever lease violation they have committed, and the consequences if such behavior continues.

Pests

Most common pest complaint is roaches, mice and bed bugs. First make sure that you begin with no pests. Call a contractor or maintenance person. Have the contractor or maintance person determine who or what is the cause of the pests.

How to Handle Tenant Complaints

If it is the resident, let them know that it is a violation of their lease and they may have to pay for future pest removal.

Plumbling

The most common plumbing complaint is a toilet clog. Have a maintance person or a contractor repair the clog. Sometimes tenant flush things like diapers and other inappropriate things down the toilet. Make sure that your lease agreement forbids such behavior.

Temperature Control

Have your maintenance person check the temperature. Many states have regulations on temperature, so you might want to invest in temperature lock out devices that don't allow the tenant to set the temperature.

How to Handle Tenant Complaints

Appliances

A refrigerator, stove or dish washer are the most common appliance complaints. Refrigerator repairs have priority, because food can spoil.

Hire a good appliance repair man. A repair can often save a fortune compared to a replacement.

Grounds

Getting a roof leak, a full dumpster, grass cut or snow removal is a common complaint. If you have these jobs contracted out, request a before and after photo of work done. Ice is particularly dangerous. You could get sued if someone injures themselves slipping on your property. Make sure you have reliable snow removal in place. Your maintenance team or a contractor should be able to handle most complaints about the grounds.

How to Handle Tenant Complaints

Preventative Maintenance & Summary

Have maintenance outlined in your lease. This will assist you in preventive maintenance.

* Remember, everything must be in writing.

* The complaint must be in writing.

* You must respond in writing.

* When will the work be done.

* Who will be doing the work.

* Tenants will not be allowed to select a contractor.

* No repair work will be done without your authorization.

* No verbal agreements.

* Document multiple request for the same work to help reduce frivoulous calls and requests.

* State that the request gives you permission to enter the property.

Dealing With Problem Tenants

"If you are brave enough to say goodbye, life will reward you with a new hello."

Paulo Coelho

Tenant Problems

No matter how good a job you do screening you still may come across a problem tenant. Sometimes a tenant might lose a job or have a death in the family. Something that changes their ability to meet their lease requirements. Here are some tenant problems you need to be prepared for.

Not Paying Rent

You are running a for profit business not a charity, and the rent must be paid in order for you to sustain your business. So when rent is missed what should you do? Follow the process. Each state has a legal process to follow. In some states, you serve a 3 day notice to evict. Followed by a court date. Every state has their own process. Learn your state's process and follow it to the letter.

Dealing With Problem Tenants

"It's not you, it's me..."

Structure your lease so that if you have a problem tenant you can send a notice to vacate by a certain date. Some landlords have to serve a notice to cease the violation before they can send a notice to vacate. So begin by making sure your lease is structured properly in the first place.

Probable reasons to call it quits with a tenant.

* Abusing The Dwelling

* Disturbing the peace and quiet

* Breaking occupant rules

It is much easier to remove a tenant that has not paid, then a tenant that is breaking lease laws. So make sure your lease is very detailed as to what the rules are and what will happen if the rules are broken.

Chapter 7
End Vacancy Worries: Marketing for Vacancy

Marketing for Vacancy

The first part to marketing for vacancy is to reduce the chance of vacancy in the first place. Treat the tenants you have to your highest level of customer service.

Begin by having a scheduled visit at least once a year. During the visit talk to the tenant and ask them what you can do to make their stay in your property better. Make sure that when you schedule the visit you have also scheduled some form of improvement to the property. Let them see you caring for them with action, not just words. Change the air filter, paint a room, replace an appliance.

Give gifts. Offer your tenants referral fees. Let them know that it's something in it for them if they help keep your properties rented. Give your tenants a movie gift certificate for a family night out. Give the tenant a turkey or ham during the holidays, along with a thank you card, showing how much you appreciate their business. How much does a turkey cost? How much does one month of a vacant property cost?

If you are renting single family homes, offer a "rent to own" contract. Usually lasting two to three years. This gives the renter time to save money and establish credit.

Offer rent incentives for the tenant to stay longer. For example, a twelve month lease is $800 a month, a eighteen month lease is $775 a month, a twenty four month lease is $750 a month.

Now that you have done all that you can to treat the tenants you have properly, you have to focus on filling vacant rental property.

Begin by viewing the federal fair housing act of 1968. Make sure that your ads or policies are not in violation of this law. You can view this document at this web site.

Https:www.hud.gov/

Then type "fair housing" in the search box.

Begin with the new basics in the age of the internet. Create a web site. Over %70 of people looking for a place to stay, begin online. Have a well written ad.

AIDA copy writing marketing formula. Get their **Attention** with a good headline. Increase their **Desire** and **Interest** with good benefits. Initiate Action with a call to **Action**.

Have all the detailed information abut your rental property on the web site. Have good clear photographs.

Marketing for Vacancy

Create a video of your property. If possible shoot a well lit clear video tour of your property. Have your address and location, your phone number and list all unit amenities. Show the rent, the deposit required and any additional charges. This will reduce phone calls and unnecessary questions.

Begin advertising your vacancy before it is vacant. Start advertising your rental property as soon as you are given notice of a lease ending.

Place a sign on the property, letting everybody know there is a place available for rent. Have a web site address on the sign for more information.

Use internet listing services. Here are a few of the top services.

HotPads

HotPads is a map-based rental property & real estate marketplace. They have been around for over a decade. They began in November 2005. The site allows users to search for housing using an interactive map.

Https://hotpads.com/

Craigslist

Craigslist is an American nationwide classified advertisements web site with sections devoted to jobs, housing and a variety of things. They get up to 50 million views each month.

Https://craigslist.org

Cozy

The Cozy web site is an amazing utility for your rental property business. It allows you to set up rent collection, tenant screening, place property listings, rental applications, estimate rent, insurance, expense tracking and maintenance.

Http://goo.gl/gEu5Ey

Zillow Rental Manager

The Zillow rental manager is a great place for extending your education in the Rental Property Business. The resource section of the Zillow Rental Manager has information on becoming a landlord, managing your rental, landlord laws and regulations, webinars, and tools and forms.

Https://www.zillow.com/rental-manager/

Marketing for Vacancy

Use newspapers. Another way to increase your property exposure is to place ads in newspapers, but only if you are getting a good advertising rate. Papers can be expensive and news paper circulation is dropping, but if you are the only fish in a small pond, you get all the attention.

Use Google. Use Google to search for local rental property. See where your competitors are advertising for tenants. Duplicate some or all of the places they are advertising.

Use local library and college bulletin boards. Place a three by five card or a business card with your web site and contact information on it.

Use word of mouth. Carry business cards to give away to family and friends or associates at networking events.

In summary, do the best you can to keep the tenants you have. Set up a web site that has as much detailed information as possible, allowing you to qualify tenants without wasting your time. Use renta listing services and local advertising to maximize exposure to your property and end any vacancy as quickly as possible.

CHAPTER 8
Business
Insurance

Consult an attorney for any and all of your business matters.

In the early 1990's an elderly woman purchased a hot cup of coffee from a McDonald's drive-thru window in Albuquerque. She spilled the coffee, and suffered 3rd degree burns. She sued Mcdonald's and won. She won 2.7 million dollars in a punitive damages victory. The verdict was appealed and settlement is estimated at somewhere in the neighborhood of $500,000 dollars. All because she spilled the coffee into her lap, while trying to add sugar and cream.

Two men in Ohio, were carpet layers. They were severely burned when a three and a half gallon container of carpet adhesive ignited, when the hot water heater it was sitting next to, was turned on. They felt the warning lable on the back of the can was insufficient. So they filed a lawsuit against the adhesive manufacturers and were awarded nine million dollars.

A woman in Oklahoma, purchased a brand new Winnebago. While driving it home, she set the cruise control to 70 miles per hour. She then left the drivers seat to make some coffee or a sandwich in the back of the motor home.

The vehicle crashed and the woman sued Winnebago for not advising her, that cruise control does not drive and steer the vehicle. She won 1.7 million dollars and the company had to rewrite their instruction manual.

Unfortunately all three outrageous lawsuits are real. If you are going to run a business, any business, you should consider protecting yourself with Professional Liability Insurance, also known as Errors and Omissions (E & 0) insurance.

This type of insurance can help to protect you from having to pay the full cost of defending yourself against a negligence lawsuit claim.

Error and Omissions can protect you against claims that are not usually covered in regular liability insurance. Those policies usually cover bodily harm, or damage to property. Error and Omissions can protect you agaist negligence, and other mental anguish like inaccurate advice, or misrepresentation. Criminal prosecution is not covered.

Errors and Ommision insurance is recommended for notaries public, real estate brokers or investors and professionals like: software engineers, lawyers, home inspectors web site delvelopers and landscape architects to name a few professions.

The Most Common Errors and Omission Claims:

%25 Breach of Fiduciary Duty

%15 Breach of Contract

%14 Negligence

%13 Failure to Supervise

%11 Unsuitability

%10 Other

BUSINESS INSURANCE

Things you should know about or require before purchasing a Errors and Omission policy is...

* What is the limit of liability

* What is the Deductible

* Does it include FDD First Dollar Defense - which obligates the insurance company to fight a case without a deductible first.

* Do I have Tail-end coverage or Extended Reporting Coverage (insurance that lasts into retirement)

* Extended coverage for Employees

* Cyber Liability Coverage

* Department of Labor Fiduciary Coverage

* Insolvency Coverage

If you get Errors and Omission insurance, renew it the day it expires. You must be careful to avoid gaps in your coverage, or it could result in not getting you policy renewed.

A few E & O Insurance Providers:

Insureon

Insureon states that their median Errors and Omissions Insurance policy cost about $750 a year or about $65 a month. The price of course will vary according to your business, the policy you choose and other risk factors.

https://www.insureon.com/home

EOforless

EOforless.com helps insurance, investment, and real estate professionals buy E & O insurance at an affordable cost in five minutes or less.

https://www.eoforless.com/

CalSurance Associates

As a leading insurance broker, CalSurance Associates
a division of Brown & Brown Program Insurance
Services, Inc. has over fifty years of experience
delivering comprehensive insurance products,
exceptional service, and proven results to over
150,000 insured. They provide professionals
nationwide and across multiple industries, including
some of the largest financial firms and insurance
companies in the United States.

http://www.calsurance.com/csweb/index.aspx

Better Safe Than Sorry

Insurance is one of the hidden costs of doing
business. These are just a few companies and a
brief overview on the topic of business insurance.
Make sure to talk to an attorney or quailified
insurance agent before making any decision on
insurance. Protect you and your business. Many
states do not require E & O insurances. But when yo
see the cost of some of the settlements, it's better to
be safe than sorry.

Chapter 9

Rehabbing Real Estate

Rehabbing Real Estate

There are three basic components to rehabbing a property. Have a property inspection, a cost analysis and hire a contractor.

A. Home Inspection

You can hire a licensed professional to inspect the propery or you can do it yourself. I advise hiring a licensed professional with a great deal of experience.

To hire a professional you can google "home inspection, your city, your state" or go to homeadvisor.com.

http://www.homeadvisor.com/

https://goo.gl/vL4gWK

If you choose to do it yourself here is a basic home inspection checklist.

Rehabbing Real Estate

Exterior

* **Roof:** Determine if the roof needs repairs or needs to be replaced.

* **Lawn:** Determine what kind of landscaping is needed or if the yard needs to be reseeded.

* **Sprinkler:** Is there a sprinkler system? If so does it work?

* **Lights:** Do the lights work? Are there motion sensors? Are there cost efficient bulbs?

* **Outlets:** Do the outlets work?

* **Fence:** Does it need repair or painting?

* **Trees:** Do any trees need to be removed or trimmed?

* **Garage Door:** Does it open and close easily?

Rehabbing Real Estate

Overall Interior

* **Walls:** Do they need paint or repair?

* **Floors:** Do tiles or carpet need to be replaced? Do wood floors need to be repaired?

* **Stairs:** Are the stairs sturdy? Do they make noise. Is the handrail sturdy and safe?

***Outlets:** Purchase a voltage tester and see if all the outlets work.

* **Doors:** Do they open and close easily? Are they level?

***Windows:** Do you feel any breezes when you stand by them? Are they cost efficient?

***Lights:** Turn on every light switch to make sure they work. (Note: If the home is unoccupied and the power is turned off, this won't be possible.)

Kitchen

* **Countertops:** Check for chips and cracks.

* **Cabinets:** Do they open and close easily? Do they need to be refinished or replaced?

* **Oven:** Does the oven work? Is it outdated

* **Refrigerator:** Check to see if it freezes. Does it pass the eyeball test or is it an eyesore.

* **Faucet:** Run the water in the sink. Any leaks? How is the water pressure?

* **Range Hood:** See if the range hood fan and light work. It most likely will need to be cleaned.

Rehabbing Real Estate

Bathrooms

* Plumbing/Drainage: Fill up the sink and tub and see how the water drains out.

* Faucets: Check for leaks.

* Toilet: Is there enough pressure when it is flushed?

* Bath Tub: Is it too small? Any scratches?

* Ventilation: Does the fan work? Is there a window? Does it open and close easily?

Bedrooms

* Closets: Is there enough space? Are hanger rods needed?

Living/Dining/Family Room

* Ceiling Fans: Do ceiling fans need to be added or replaced?

Basement

* Mold: If there is an odor, check for mold and mildew.

* Furnace: Does the furnace work? Is it outdated? Up to code?

* Water Heater: Check for water around the base of the water heater. Any stickers on this to indicate installation date?

A documentary about Walt Disney revealed that Walt purchased a home for his parents and a faulty gas furnace was the cause of his mother's death. So inspecting a house can be a life or death matter.

You can use this checklist to determine your offer price and begin a overall cost analysis. However it is highly recommended that you use a professional.

B. Cost Analysis

When investing in real estate, you should always stack the numbers in your favor. If you can purchase a property at %50 of it's wholesale value, then you leave enough margin for error to absorb expenses and still sell the property for a profit.

The real estate web site biggerpockets.com has a investment calculator that can do the cost analysis work for you.

https://www.biggerpockets.com/real-estate-investment-calculator

https://goo.gl/HFoK9x

However you can do a quick cost analysis yourself. Here are the basic numbers you will need.

* after repair value

* desired profit

* estimated repair cost

* purchase closing cost

* sale closing cost

* agent commission

* monthly holding costs

* number of days it will take to rehab and sell

Take the "after repair value" and substract all of the expenses.

C. Hire a Contractor

It is a good idea that you hire a contractor. However if you decide to do the repair work yourself there is a supply discount program from Home Depot.

WHAT IS IT?

You have to get their Pro Xtra Account. If you're spending at least $1,500, chances are you can save money. In select markets, you may only need to spend only $1,000. Check with your local store to confirm required purchase amount.

HOW DOES IT WORK?

Assemble your project list. Build your cart in the store. If your total adds up to at least $1,500 (or $1,000 in select markets, check with your local store), you probably qualify for a volume discount.

Quotes can be processed by the Pro Desk any time and most requests are priced immediately. Membership in Pro Xtra Loyalty Program is required to receive discounts.

Full details are at the web site listed below...

http://www.homedepot.com/c/Pro_VolumePricing

A. How to Find a good Contractor

Go to your local building material warehouses like Lowes, Home Depot, Menards and Sherwin Williams.

Ask them who are their high volume contractors. If contracters are frequently purchasing supplies then they are frequently working. This is one of the more reliable ways to find a quality contractor.

Ask other contractors. Often times you will come across a good contractor who is busy on another project. Ask him/her for recommendations.

Ask a high volume real estate agent. Top real estate agents usually know one or two good contractors.

Use the internet.

Google "contractors, your city, your state".

Use homeadvisor.com

Try angieslist.com

B. Contractor Checklist

Hiring the right contractor can make or break a deal. Remember they work for you, so don't be shy about asking questions and getting proof, BEFORE you sign a contract. Here is a question checklist.

1. Do you have a license bond and insurance?

Do You Carry General Liability Insurance?

- It is Best to find a remodel contractor that carries general liability insurance.

2. Do you have referrals?

Do not hesitate to call referrals. - Nice to get several customer references from the last 6 months to one year.

3. Can I get a detailed and comprehensive scope of work with the bid?

4. Ask about experience and verify if you can.

5. Who's doing the work and who's going to be the daily contact on the project?

- Make sure the contractor or his foreman is on the job whenever work is being performed.

6. Will You Pull All the Required Building Permits?

- Pulling the required building permits, you know things will be done to "code."

7. Do You Guarantee Your Work?

Your contractor should guarantee his work for at least one year from date of completion. They should also include any warranties from the material used if applicable.

8. How do you handle clean up?

Clean up can be expensive. You need to know if the best options are being used.

9. How Is Payment Handled?

- Per job?

- Upon completion?

- Weekly?

- Some money upfront?

- Do you have capital to buy materials in case we need you to?

These are basic questions that you should be asking to interview contractors before you begin any job. Hiring the right contractor can go a long way in giving you peace of mind, when you are a Real Estate investor.

Chapter 10

Millionaire Real Estate Rolodex

Get Started Fast with these Business Web Sites

As of the writing of this book, all of the companies web site's are up and running. From time to time companies go out of business or change their web address. So, instead of just giving you just 1 source I give you plenty of sources to choose from.

Top 15 Most Popular eBizMBA Rank

Real Estate Websites

with Estimated Unique Monthly Visitors

1. **Zillow**   36,000,000

2. **Trulia**   23,000,000

3. **Yahoo! Homes**   20,000,000

4. **Realtor**   18,000,000

5. **Redfin**   6,000,000

6. **Homes**   5,000,000

MILLIONAIRE ROLODEX

Top 15 Most Popular eBizMBA Rank

Real Estate Websites	Monthly Visitors
7. ApartmentGuide	2,500,000
8. Curbed	2,000,000
9. ReMax	1,800,000
10. HotPads	1,750,000
11. ZipRealty	1,600,000
12. Apartments	1,500,000
13. Rent	1,400,000
14. Auction	1,300,000
15. ForRent	1,200,000

Nationwide Banks & Foreclosure Properties

Bank of America

http://foreclosures.bankofamerica.com/

Wells Fargo

https://reo.wellsfargo.com/

Ocwen Financial Corporation

http://www.ocwen.com/reo

Hubzu

http://www.hubzu.com/

Government Foreclosure Properties

Fannie Mae
The Federal National Mortgage Association

https://www.fanniemae.com/singlefamily/reo-vendors

Department of Housing and Urban Development

https://www.hudhomestore.com/Home/Index.aspx

The Federal Deposit Insurance Corporation

https://www.fdic.gov/buying/owned/

The United States Department of Agriculture

https://properties.sc.egov.usda.gov/resales/index.jsp

United States Marshals

https://www.usmarshals.gov/assets/sales.htm#real_estate

Commercial Real Estate Properties

City Feet

http://www.cityfeet.com/#

The Commercial Real Estate Listing Service

https://www.cimls.com/

Land . Net

http://www.land.net/

Loop . Net

http://www.loopnet.com/

FSBO – For Sale By Owner Properties

By Owner

http://www.byowner.com/

For sale by owner in Canada

http://www.fsbo-bc.com/

For sale by owner Central

http://www.fsbocentral.com/

For sale by Owner: world's largest FSBO web site

http://www.forsalebyowner.com/

Ranch by owner

http://www.ranchbyowner.com/

Tools to Get You Started Video Marketing

https://www.YouTube.com/

Upload your videos to this web site.

https://www.wikipedia.org/

Get valuable information for video topics.

https://screencast-o-matic.com/

Use this screen capture software to create videos

http://www.openoffice.org/download/

Use this Open source word processor software to make slides for your videos.

Free Keyword Tools

Google keyword planner

https://adwords.google.com/home/tools/keyword-planner/

SEO Centro

http://www.seocentro.com/

Ubersuggest

https://ubersuggest.io/

Promoting Your Real Estate/Videos

Top Free Press Release Websites

https://www.prlog.org

https://www.pr.com

https://www.pr-inside.com

https://www.newswire.com

https://www.OnlinePRNews.com

MILLIONAIRE ROLODEX

Top Social Media Websites

https://www.facebook.com

https://www.tumbler.com

https://www.pinterest.com

https://www.reddit.com

https://www.linkedin.com/

http://digg.com/

https://twitter.com

https://instagram.com

For Everything Under the Sun at Wholesale Prices

http://www.liquidation.com/

COMPUTERS/Office Equipment

http://www.wtsmedia.com/

http://www.laptopplaza.com/

http://www.outletpc.com/

With this "Millionaire Rolodex" of real estate business resources, you have a ton of web sites that you can use to get started working on your real estate business with little to no money.

So take advantage of these resources to continue to gain valuable knowledge, save money and promote your real estate business.

Chapter 11

REAL ESTATE
DEFINITIONS

Acceleration Clause - A contract provision that allows a lender to require a borrower to repay all or part of an outstanding loan if certain requirements are not met. An acceleration clause outlines the reasons that the lender can demand loan repayment Also known as "acceleration covenant".

Active Income - Active income is income for which services have been performed. This includes wages, tips, salaries, commissions and income from businesses in which there is material participation.

Agent - One who is legally authorized to act on behalf of another person.

All-inclusive deed of trust (AITD) - An All Inclusive Trust Deed (AITD) is a new deed of trust that includes the balance due on the existing note plus new funds advanced; also known as a wrap-around mortgage.

Amortized loan - An amortized loan is a loan with scheduled periodic payments that consist of both principal and interest. An amortized loan payment pays the relevant interest expense for the period before any principal is paid and reduced.

Real Estate Definitions

Appraiser - A practitioner who has the knowledge and expertise necessary to estimate the value of an asset, or the likelihood of an event occurring, and the cost of such an occurrence.

Asking price - the price at which something is offered for sale.

Assignment - An assignment (Latin cessio) is a term used with similar meanings in the law of contracts and in the law of real estate. In both instances, it encompasses the transfer of rights held by one party—the assignor—to another party—the assignee.

At-risk rule - Tax laws limiting the amount of losses an investor (usually a limited partner) can claim. Only the amount actually at risk can be deducted.

Balloon mortgage - a mortgage in which a large portion of the borrowed principal is repaid in a single payment at the end of the loan period.

Capital gain - a profit from the sale of property or of an investment.

Cash flow - the total amount of money being transferred into and out of a business, especially as affecting liquidity.

Real Estate Definitions

Chattel - an item of property other than real estate.

Co-insurance - a type of insurance in which the insured pays a share of the payment made against a claim.

Contract of sale - A real estate contract is a contract between parties for the purchase and sale, exchange, or other conveyance of real estate.

Declining balance method - A declining balance method is a common depreciation-calculation system that involves applying the depreciation rate against the non-depreciated balance.

Depreciation - Depreciation is an accounting method of allocating the cost of a tangible asset over its useful life. Businesses depreciate long-term assets for both tax and accounting purposes.

Earnest money - Earnest money is a deposit made to a seller showing the buyer's good faith in a transaction. Often used in real estate transactions, earnest money allows the buyer additional time when seeking financing. Earnest money is typically held jointly by the seller and buyer in a trust or escrow account.

Real Estate Definitions

Equity participation - Equity participation is the ownership of shares in a company or property. ... The greater the equity participation rate, the higher the percentage of shares owned by stakeholders. Allowing stakeholders to own shares ties the stakeholders' success with that of the company or real estate investment.

Estoppel - Estoppel Certificate. An estoppel certificate is a document used in mortgage negotiations to establish facts and financial obligations, such as outstanding amounts due that can affect the settlement of a loan. It is required by a lender of a third party in a real estate transaction.

Fee simple - In English law, a fee simple or fee simple absolute is an estate in land, a form of freehold ownership. It is a way that real estate may be owned in common law countries, and is the highest possible ownership interest that can be held in real property.

Gift deed - Quitclaim Deed Vs. Gift Deed. Property deeds define and protect ownership in a home. In real estate, deeds are legal documents that transfer ownership of a property from one party to another. ... Each type of deed is used for a specific situation.

Real Estate Definitions

Gross income - A real estate investment term, Gross Operating Income refers to the result of subtracting the credit and vacancy losses from a property's gross potential income. Also Known As: Effective Gross Income (EGI)

Income approach to value - The income approach is a real estate appraisal method that allows investors to estimate the value of a property by taking the net operating income of the rent collected and dividing it by the capitalization rate.

Interest - Estates and ownership interests defined. The law recognizes different sorts of interests, called estates, in real property. The type of estate is generally determined by the language of the deed, lease, bill of sale, will, land grant, etc., through which the estate was acquired.

Joint and several note - Joint and several note is a promissory note which is the note of all and of each of the makers as to its legal obligation between the parties to it.

Real Estate Definitions

Lease option - A lease option (more formally Lease With the Option to Purchase) is a type of contract used in both residential and commercial real estate. In a lease-option, a property owner and tenant agree that, at the end of a specified rental period for a given property, the renter has the option of purchasing the property.

Like kind property - Like-Kind Property. Any two assets or properties that are considered to be the same type, making an exchange between them tax free. To qualify as like kind, two assets must be of the same type (e.g. two pieces of residential real estate), but do not have to be of the same quality.

Loan to value - The loan to value or LTV ratio of a property is the percentage of the property's value that is mortgaged. ... Loan to Value is used in commercial real estate as well. Examples: $300,000 appraised value of a home. $240,000 mortgage on the property. $240,000 / $300,000 = .80 or 80% Loan to Value Ratio

Mortgage broker - A mortgage broker is an intermediary working with a borrower and a lender while qualifying the borrower for a mortgage. The broker gathers income, asset and employment documentation, a credit report and other information for assessing the borrower's ability to secure financing.

Real Estate Definitions

Net rentable area - Actual square-unit of a building that may be leased or rented to tenants, the area upon which the lease or rental payments are computed. It usually excludes common areas, elevator shafts, stairways, and space devoted to cooling, heating, or other equipment. Also called net leasable area.

Option - A real estate purchase option is a contract on a specific piece of real estate that allows the buyer the exclusive right to purchase the property. Once a buyer has an option to buy a property, the seller cannot sell the property to anyone else.

Possession - A principle of real estate law that allows a person who possesses someone else's land for an extended period of time to claim legal title to that land.

Prepayment penalty - Prepayment Penalty. A prepayment penalty is a clause in a mortgage contract stating that a penalty will be assessed if the mortgage is prepaid within a certain time period. The penalty is based on a percentage of the remaining mortgage balance or a certain number of months' worth of interest.

Real Estate Definitions

Promissory note - In the United States, a mortgage note (also known as a real estate lien note, borrower's note) is a promissory note secured by a specified mortgage loan; it is a written promise to repay a specified sum of money plus interest at a specified rate and length of time to fulfill the promise.

Real estate owned (REO) - Real estate owned or REO is a term used in the United States to describe a class of property owned by a lender—typically a bank, government agency, or government loan insurer—after an unsuccessful sale at a foreclosure auction.

Refinancing - Getting a new mortgage to replace the original is called refinancing. Refinancing is done to allow a borrower to obtain a better interest term and rate. The first loan is paid off, allowing the second loan to be created, instead of simply making a new mortgage and throwing out the original mortgage.

Reproduction cost - The costs involved with identically reproducing an asset or property with the same materials and specifications as an insured property based on current prices.

Real Estate Definitions

Right of survivorship - The right of survivorship is an attribute of several types of joint ownership of property, most notably joint tenancy and tenancy in common. When jointly owned property includes a right of survivorship, the surviving owner automatically absorbs a dying owner's share of the property. Thus if A and B jointly own a house with a right of survivorship, and B dies, A becomes the sole owner of the house, despite any contrary intent in B' will.

Standby commitment - A standby commitment is a formal agreement by a bank agreeing to lend money to a borrower up to a specified amount for a specific period. It is also known as firm commitment lending. The amount given under standby commitment is to be used only in specified contingency.

Supply and demand - The law of supply and demand is a basic economic principle that explains the relationship between supply and demand for a good or service and how the interaction affects the price of that good or service. The relationship of supply and demand affects the housing market and the price of a house

Real Estate Definitions

Tenancy by entirety - Tenants by entirety (TBE) is a method in some states by which married couples can hold the title to a property. In order for one spouse to modify his or her interest in the property in any way, the consent of both spouses is required by tenants by entirety.

Title insurance policy - Title insurance is an insurance policy that covers the loss of ownership interest in a property due to legal defects and is required if the property is under mortgage. The most common type of title insurance is a lender's title insurance, which is paid for by the borrower but protects only the lender.

Vacancy and rent loss - Vacancy and Credit Loss in real estate investing is the amount of money or percentage of net operating income that is estimated to not be realized due to non-payment of rents and vacant units

Will - A will or testament is a legal document by which a person, the testator, expresses their wishes as to how their property is to be distributed at death, and names one or more persons, the executor, to manage the estate until its final distribution.

$10,000

Massive Money Internet Marketing &

Copy Writing & SEO Course &

$1,000 Value Bonus

Internet Marketing Videos

LIBRARY I (Video Training Programs)

1. Product Creation
2. Copy Writing & Payment
3. Auto Responder & Product Download Page
4. How to start a Freelancing business
5. Video Marketing
6. List Building
7. Affiliate Marketing
8. How to Get Massive Web Site Traffic

LIBRARY II (Video Training Programs)

1. Goldmine Government Grants
2. How to Write a Business Plan
3. Secrets to making money on eBay
4. Credit Repair
5. Goal Setting
6. Asset Protection How to Incorporate

$10,000 MegaSized Internet Marketing &

Copy Writing & SEO Course &

$1,000 Value Bonus

Library III
1. SEO SIMPLIFIED PART 1
2. SEO SIMPLIFIED PART 2
3. SEO Private Network Blogs
4. SEO Social Signals
5. SEO Profits

Bonus 1000 Package!
1. Insider Secrets to Government Contracts (PDF)
2. 1000 Books/Guides (text files)
3. Vacation Discounts (text file w/links to discounts)
4. Media Players (3 Software Programs)
100% MONEY BACK GUARANTEE!!!
ALL ON A 8 GIGABYTE FLASH DRIVE

This Massive Library with a $10,000 value all for only a
1 time payment of $67!!!
Get Instant Access by Using the Link Below:

https://urlzs.com/p7v3T

Leave a review and join Our VIP Mailing List Then Get All our Audio Books Free! We will be releasing over 100 money making audio books within the next 12 months! Just leave a review and join our mailing list and get them all for free!

Just Hit/Type in the Link Below

https://urlzs.com/HfbGF